OLD BESS

Written by Cynthia S. Vander Ark

Illustrated by Audrey Savage

HOG'S BACK
MOUNTAIN

Hog's Back Mountain Publishing

Copyright © Cynthia S. Vander Ark 2023

All rights reserved. No part of this publication may be reproduced or utilized in any form or by any means, electronic or mechanical, including photocopying, or by any information storage and retrieval system, without prior written permission from the publisher.

979-8-9891789-0-2

Wendell Berry, "The Peace of Wild Things" from New Collected Poems. Copyright © 2012 by Wendell Berry. Reprinted with the permission of The Permissions Company, LLC on behalf of Counterpoint Press, counterpointpress.com.

Book design by Daniel Thomas Dyer

Printed in China

cynthiasvanderark.com

@hogsback_mountain

This book is dedicated to Andy Ide who over the last 10 years
has been helping me birth my stories with resolute kindness... this one included!

This book is also for survivors of trafficking
who are fighting daily for peace, rest and healing.

With a gentle cadence and a soul connected to the created world, Cynthia is not only the writer of this lovely story, but she's also a trustworthy guide who will take you by your hand and lead you on a search, ready to help you give birth to your stories. *Old Bess* is much more than a nighttime search for a lost cow. Along the way, readers of all ages will come face to face with their deepest longings, finding there really is a light in the darkness and someone who is looking just for you.
　~Al Andrews, author, therapist and founder of Porter's Call (www.porterscall.com)

Cynthia is a wise story doula who takes us on a risky rescue of what it means to birth hope. We all feel somewhat lost and wonder if there is hope for rescue let alone redemption. Sometimes redemption requires us to put our hands and hearts into the holy, dark places that seem too messy to enter, but those dark valleys are where we find life. This beautiful story will move you and offer a context to talk with your children about deep realities we all face in our need for care and protection. I am grateful for my friend Cynthia and I am excited to read this story to my grandchildren.
　~Rebecca Allender, author of *Hidden In Plain Sight: One Woman's Search for Identity, Intimacy and Calling*

Old Bess was missing.

She had not wandered home
with the rest of the Black Angus cows

who were peacefully chewing their cud
in their stalls.

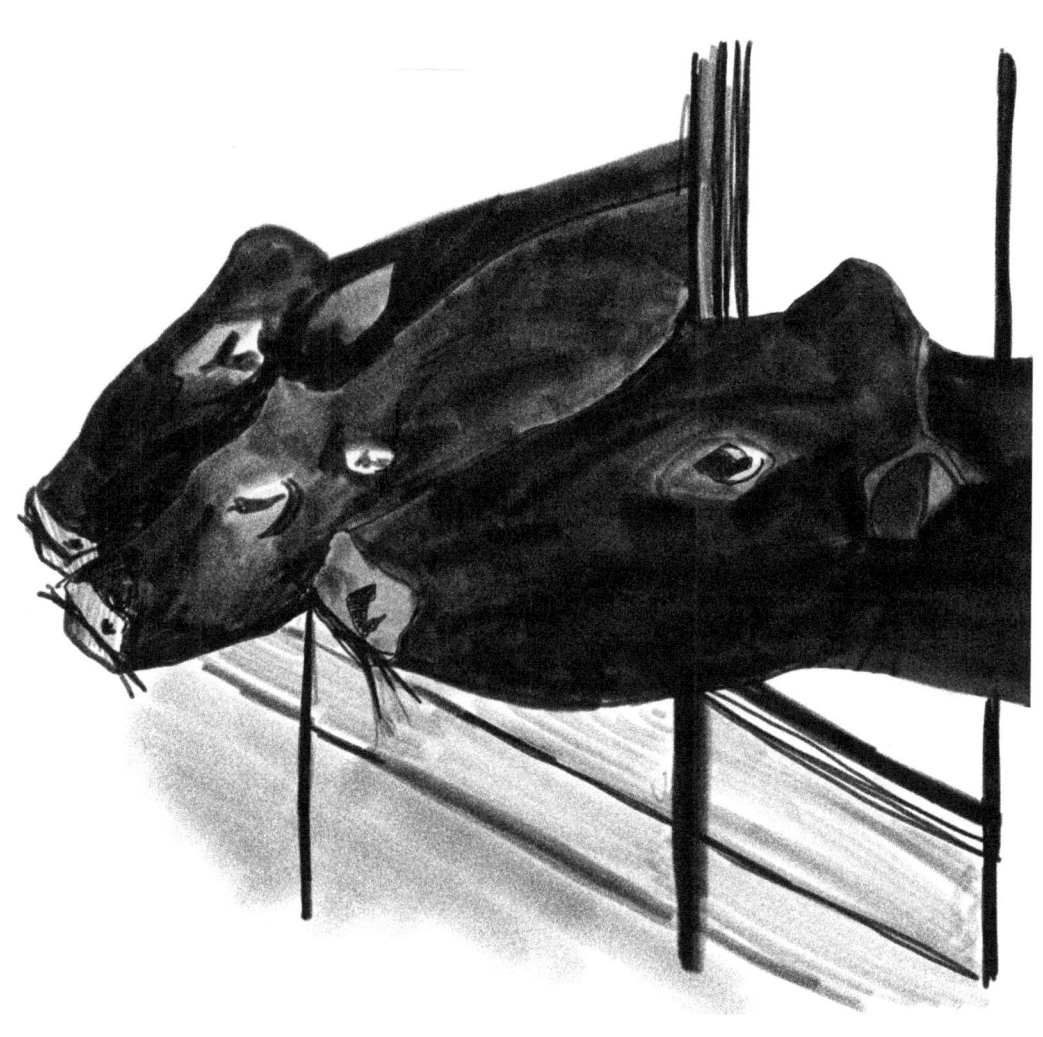

She had not come home
as the sun descended behind
Hog's Back Mountain

and the rain began to fall,
the dark storm clouds rolling closer.

Gram was worried.
Gramps was worried.

Leo, the hired hand, was worried.

Keith and I were worried,
as darkness approached.

Old Bess was very pregnant

and due to give birth that week.

She had not come home,

round and plodding, as she usually did.

Gram sent Keith and me out
and up the mountain,
searching for Old Bess.

We spread out and combed the woods, the fields, and the ravines.

We shouted,

Then we listened.

Then we hollered,

Silence...

Moans, sad and low,
stopped our calling.

Sticks cracked
and leaves crunched
beneath our feet
as we ran

and paused...

and listened...

Toward the moaning we scrambled.

Until we saw a still, dark lump,
tucked within a large hollow,

shrouded in the shadows of evening
on the forest floor.

"OLD BESS!"
She lay on her side,

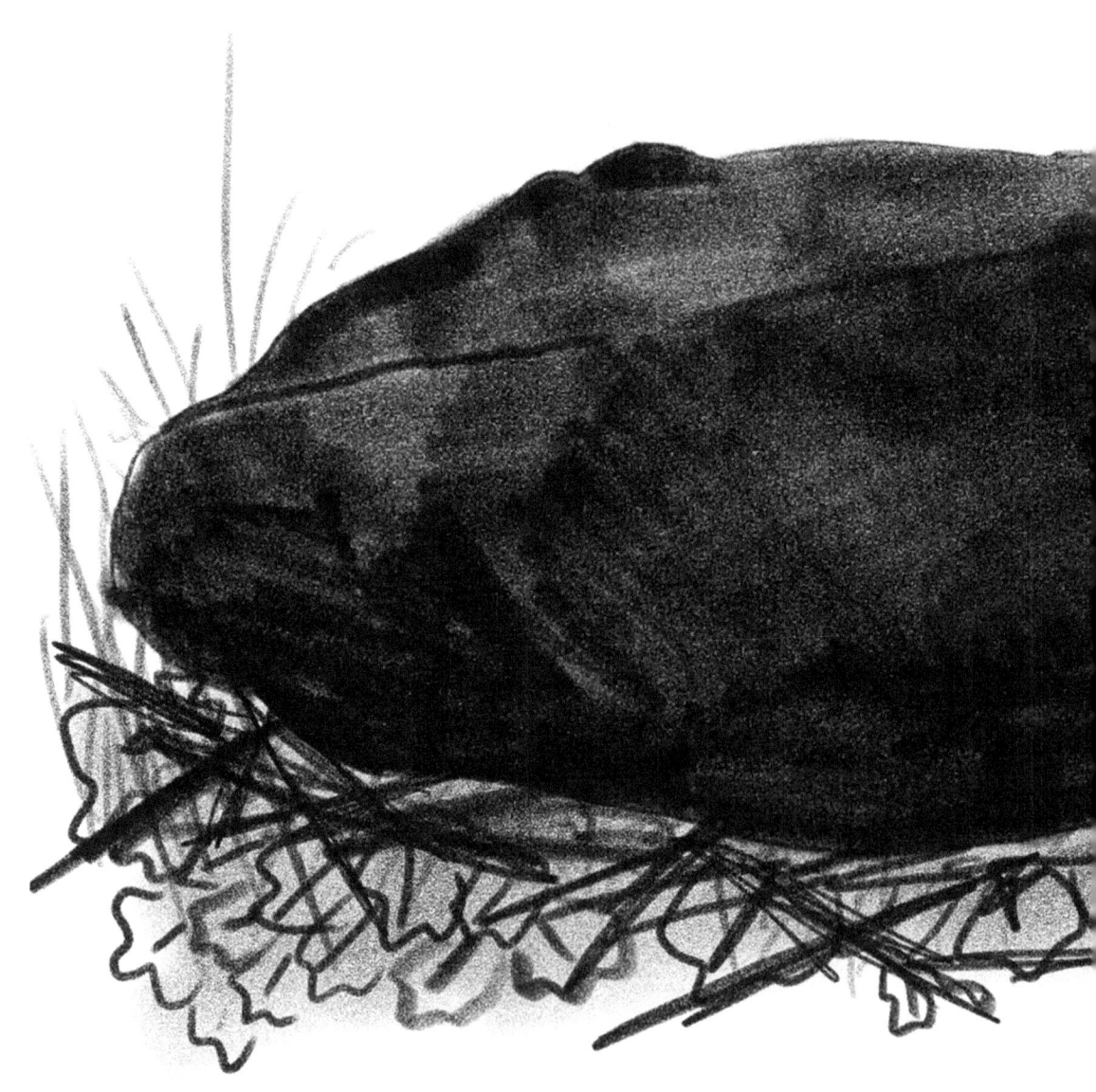

legs folded under and against her swollen middle.

She looked up as we approached.

She tried to get up to greet us,

then lay back down

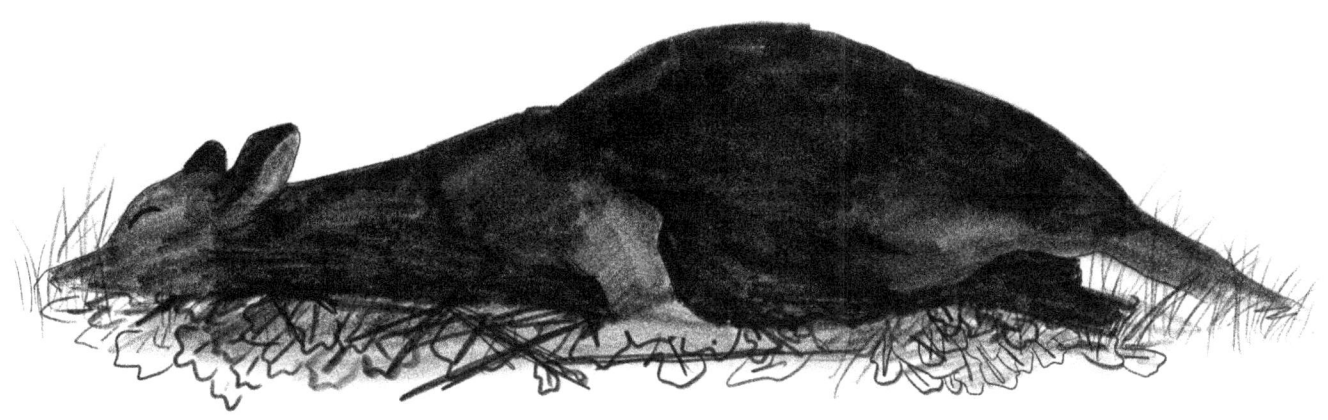

in her self-made bed of earth and leaves.

Keith ran down the mountain
to tell Gram we had found her
and to get help.

I was alone with sweet Old Bess,
and it was clear to me there was no injury
but great pain.

Something was terribly wrong.

Gram and Keith returned with ropes.

"She can't get this baby out,"
Gram said as she rolled
up her sleeves.

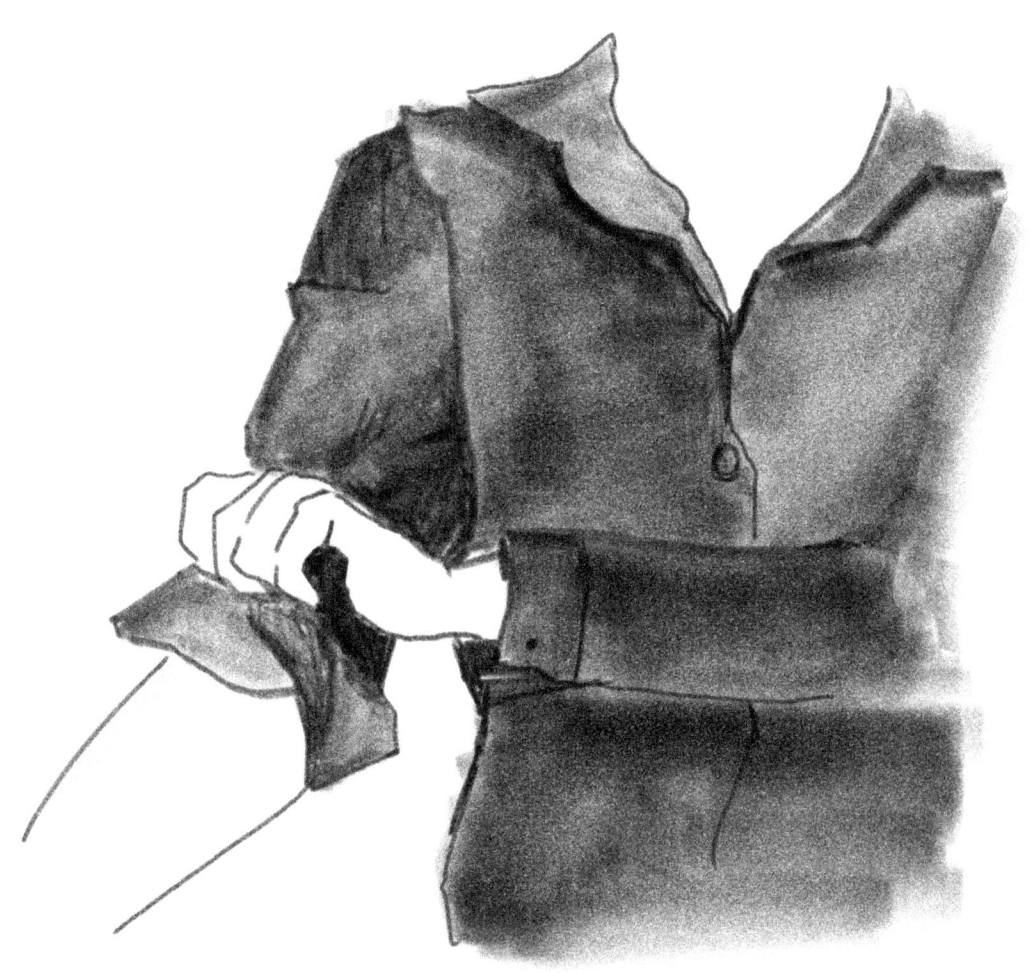

Gram inserted her whole forearm
into Old Bess's womb,
then out.

"The calf is tangled up
and backwards.
We will have to help."

She tied the rope onto
something inside Old Bess.

"Cynthia, reach your hand inside
to tighten the knot."

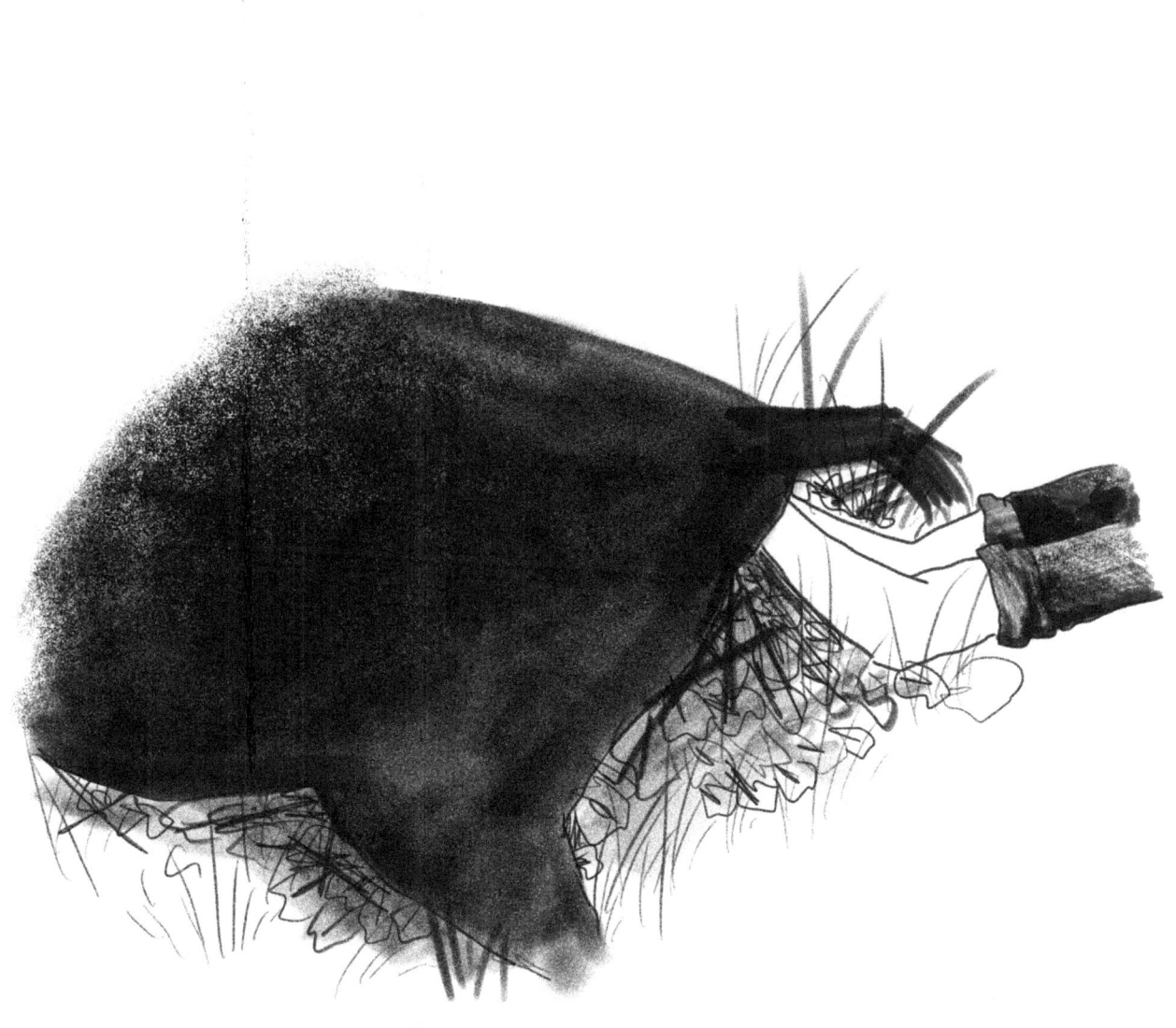

I had no choice.
I knew if I did not obey,
the calf and Old Bess would die.

In my hands went,
grabbing and tightening the rope
tied around the calf's hooves.

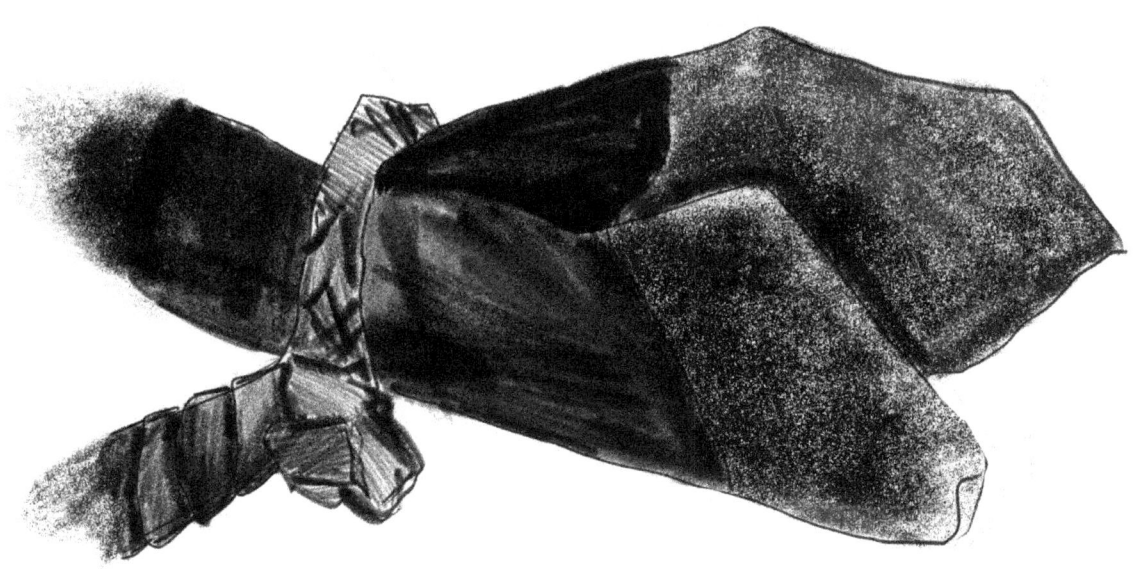

Gram held the rope on the outside.

I held the rope on the warm and slimy inside.

Keith watched from a distance.
We all waited for a contraction and a moan from Old Bess.

"GO!" said Gram, and we pulled,
inside and out.

"GO!" said Gram, and we pulled again,
inside and out.

Five times...

inside and out.

Until...

Slither and plop...

the calf slid out
onto the floor of the forest.

Old Bess, exhausted, too weak to move
and too tired to clean her calf,
laid her head down.

We let her rest for the night
in her self-made nest
of earth and leaves.

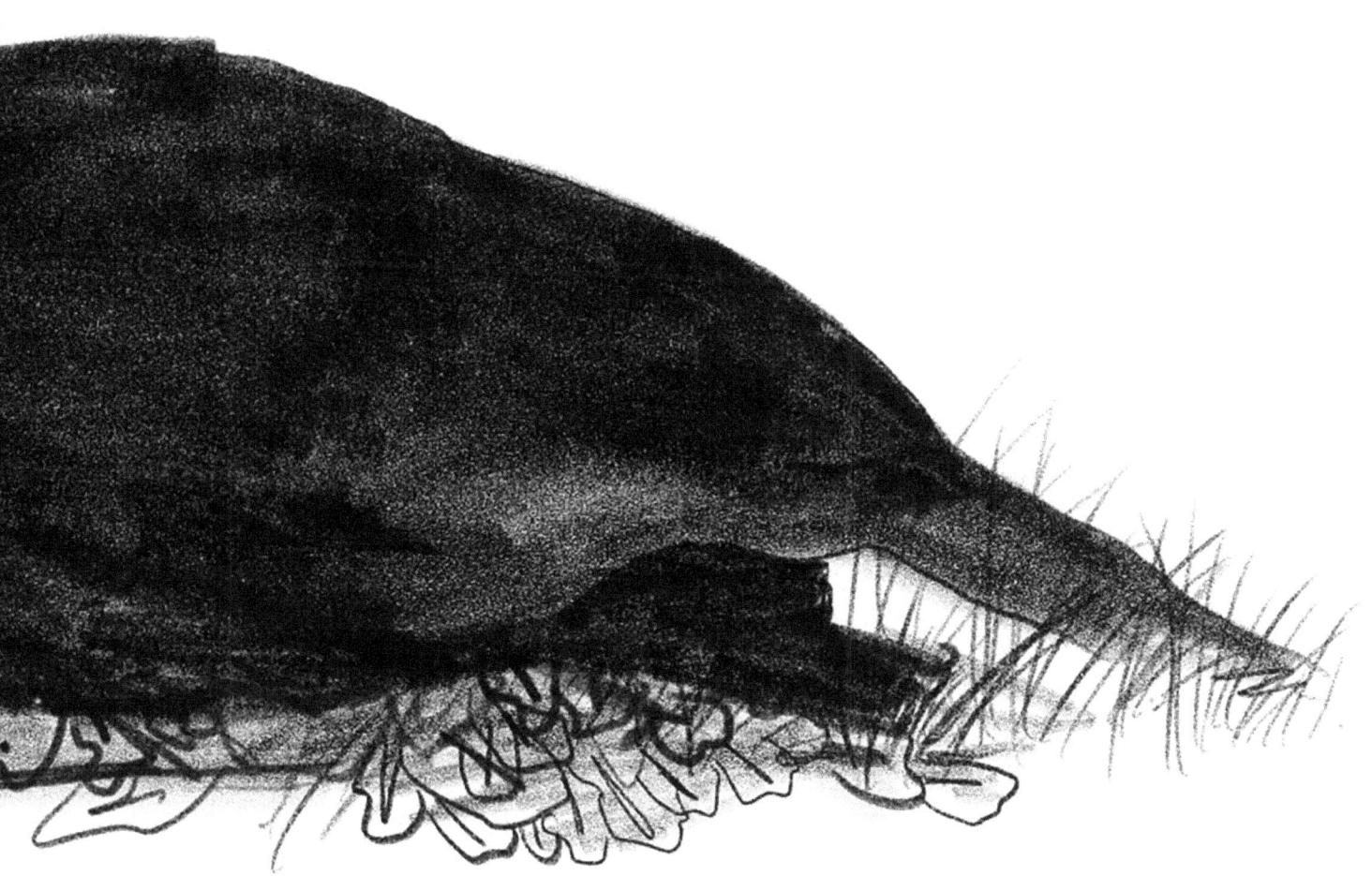

The storm continued its rumbling,
the rain continued to fall.

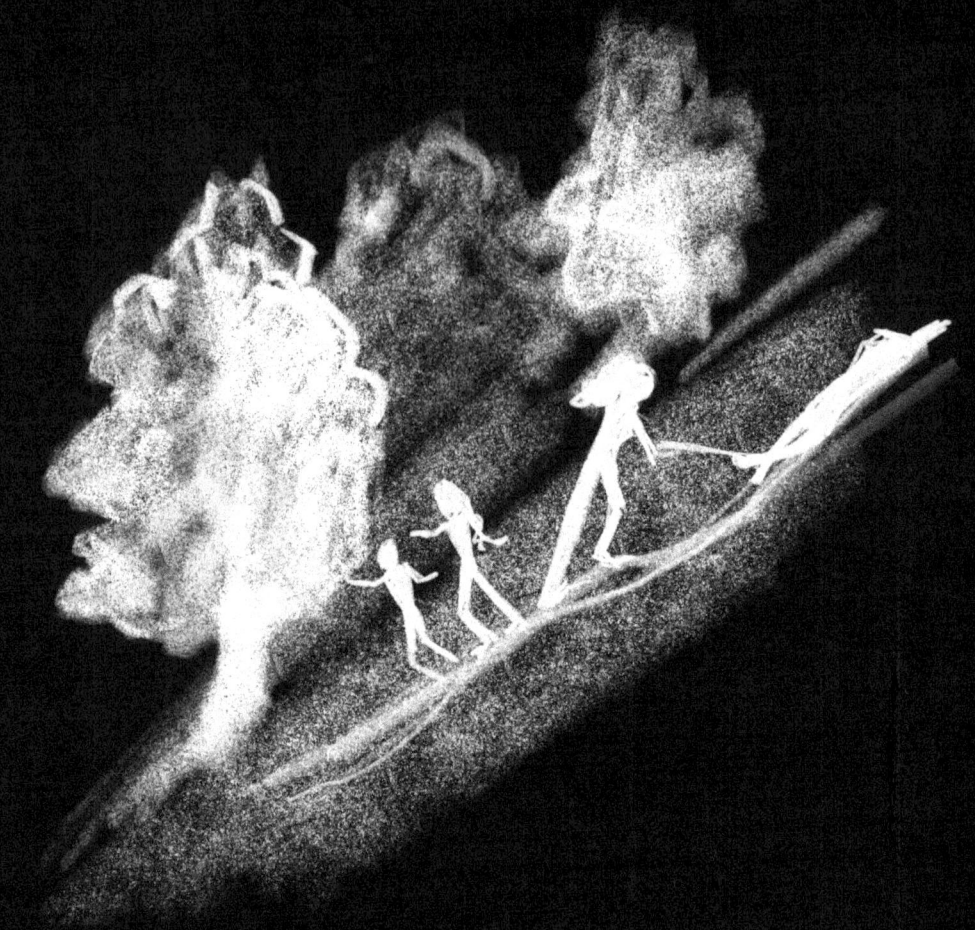

Too wobbly to walk on her own and too heavy to carry,
we carefully dragged the newborn calf
slowly down the mountain

through the leaves and the knee-high wet grass
and the shadow of nightfall

...to the old, gray clapboard barn.

I gave her warm milk from a bottle
and sighed as I nestled beside the tired newborn
and slept with her that night

in a bed of freshly laid hay,
within the comfort of rain pattering on the tin roof,

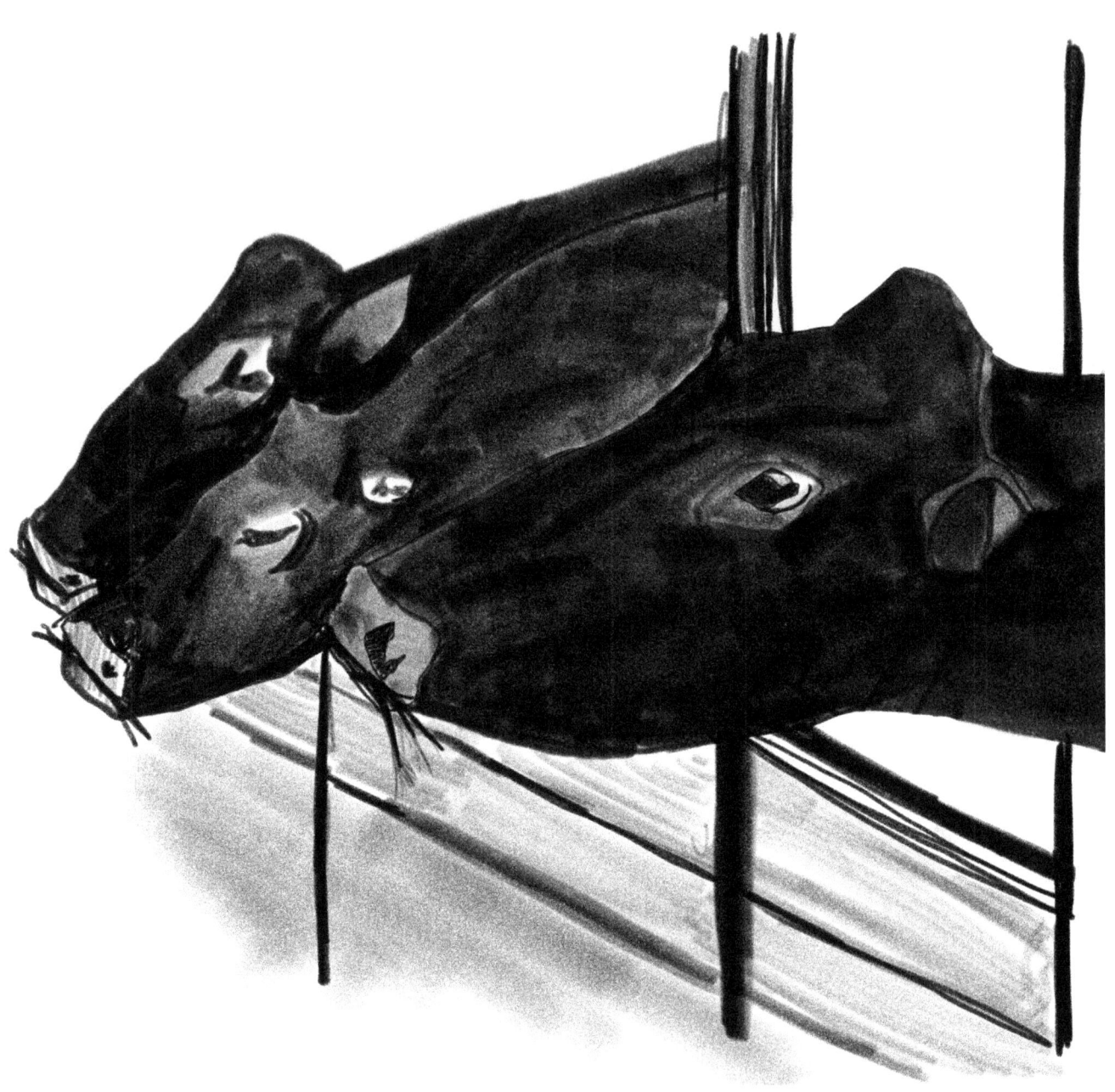

the cows' low mooing, and

the shifting of weight

as they chewed their cud

in their stalls.

As the sun began to pour its light over Hog's Back Mountain, Old Bess meandered toward home,

through the rain-soaked grass
toward the old, gray clapboard barn.

She began the job of mothering
her calf that morning...

through the dark storms and
the bright sunlight and blue skies.

It was the last one she would ever have...

before resting contentedly
the remainder of her days.

The End.

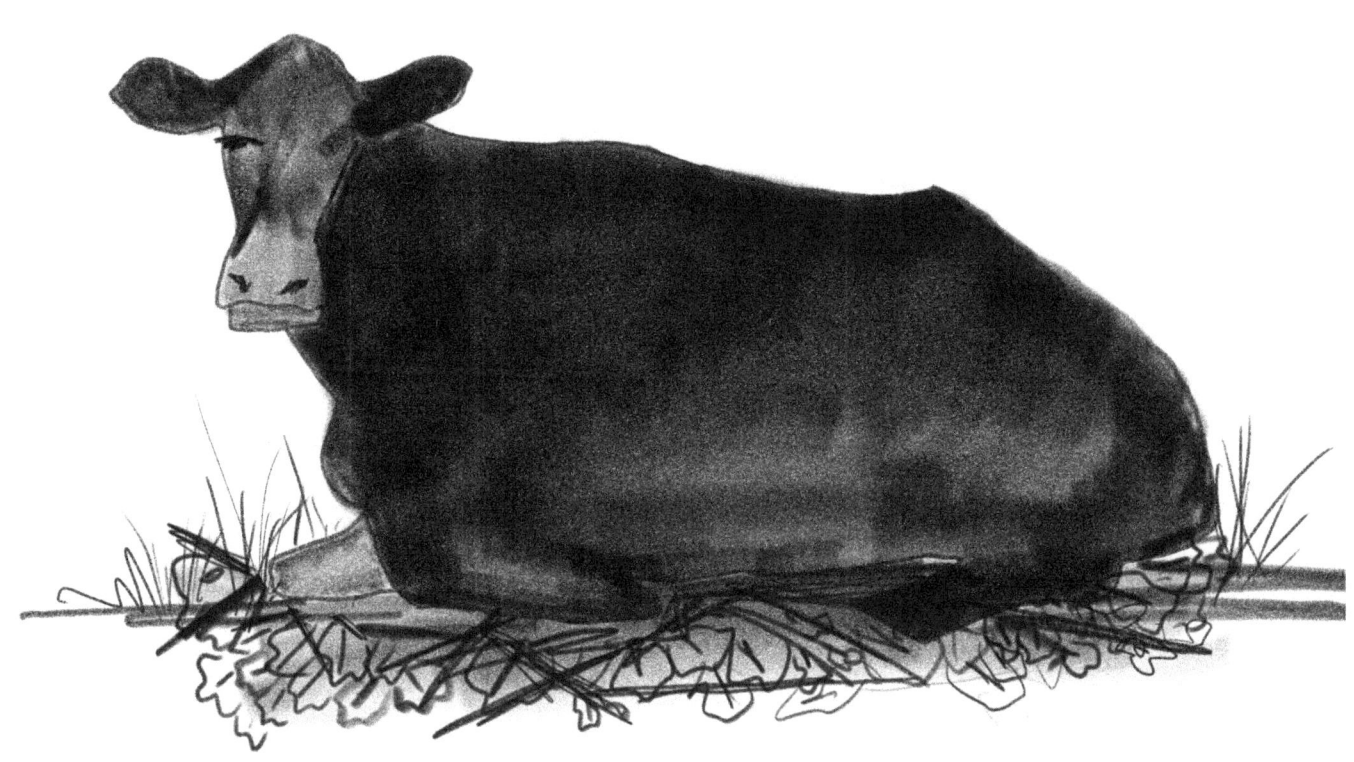

Glossary

Black Angus:
A kind of cow that originally came from Scotland. Their skin (hide) has to be at least 51% black in order to be considered a BLACK Angus.

Breech:
A baby usually comes out of the womb head first. If it is breech, then it can be upside down, backwards, or any which way! In *Old Bess*, Gram had to adjust the position of the calf with the rope so it could be born more easily.

Calf:
A baby cow. "Calf" can also be used when describing other baby mammals (elephants and whales for example).

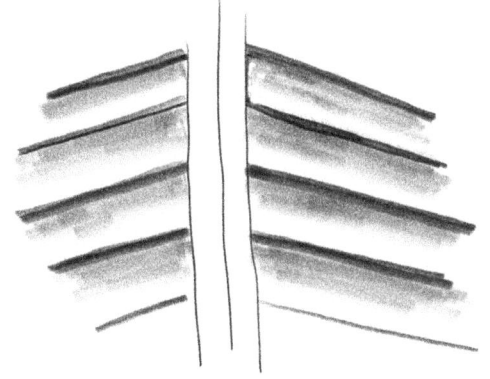

Clapboard:
Long, thin boards about 6-8 inches wide that are laid horizontally to make the outside of a structure.

Contraction:
A contraction feels like a strong cramp. It is the body's way of helping a mother push a baby out.

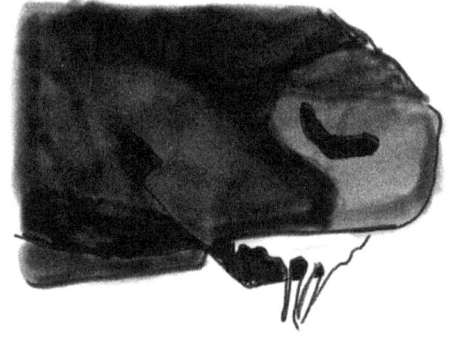

Cud:
Cows technically have one stomach, but four compartments for food. One part of the stomach is called a "rumen" where food that is partially chewed rests and bacteria helps to break it down. This food is called "cud." Cows will pull the cud back into their mouths at a later time to finish the chewing and swallow completely!

Hired hand:
Sometimes help is needed, so people pay someone (or hire them) to do extra chores. They mostly use their hands to do the work, so they are called "hired hands."

Stall:
A space in a barn where animals can sleep, rest, and take shelter.

Womb:

This is part of the female body where babies grow. For cows, the babies stay in the womb for around 283 days (about 9 months and 10 days). Like human mommies, the time can be shorter or longer.

For the Adults

The Peace of Wild Things

When despair for the world grows in me
and I wake in the night at the least sound
in fear of what my life and my children's lives may be,
I go and lie down where the wood drake
rests in his beauty on the water, and the great heron feeds.
I come into the peace of wild things
who do not tax their lives with forethought
of grief. I come into the presence of still water.
And I feel above me the day-blind stars
waiting with their light. For a time
I rest in the grace of the world, and am free.

~Wendell Berry

As I sit with this story of Old Bess, I am aware of how grateful I am for the earth and all it holds. The earth has been a wonderful and kind mother to me. God's creation has provided a place for me to know what is sure and true. It has given me a home of comfort and rest when nothing else made sense… a grounding place. As wild and unpredictable as nature can be, the earth was more dependable and much safer than my own family. I did not mind the threatening storm coming over the mountain toward us as we searched for Old Bess, nor the oncoming darkness, just as I have never feared the depths of the ocean or crashing waves as a child. I plunged into them, explored them, learned their ways. In return, I got a few tumbles, some close calls, and sheer joy in the engagement of body, soul and mind.

Keith (l) and Cynthia (r) at the end of Hog's Back Mountain.

I am reminded that God also created me as one who searches for lost things.... Not only for the lost little girl inside of myself, but for others as they come to me with their heartache and ask that I be with them like a midwife, helping them birth their stories that are stuck and breech. I have loved giving them hope that even when their stories are birthed, there may be leaves and cool, damp, grass-covered hills to be dragged through for a thorough cleansing and wakening. There may be an old clapboard barn filled with warmth and comfort and nourishment. This story of Old Bess dips into the raw and unfiltered way we all come to know ourselves. The searching, the hollering, the looming storm, the breech stories, the shadows, and redemption... a warm bottle of milk and comfort. We are all "tangled up and backwards" inside, aren't we? We are all in need of steady hands, kind words, and people to stay with us, to witness and help with the birth of babies and stories in need of tender care.

Gramma Kay walking down Hog's Back Mountain toward the farm.

Keith milking one of our Black Angus cows.

Hog's Back Mountain

cynthiasvanderark.com

@hogsback_mountain

www.ingramcontent.com/pod-product-compliance
Lightning Source LLC
Chambersburg PA
CBHW061405010526
44119CB00011B/267